Face Painting

From cowboys to clowns,
original designs for the perfect
children's party

LYNSY PINSENT

Contents

Face paints have quite magical qualities; they can completely transform someone in an instant, turning the sweetest person into an evil witch or making a plain face stunningly beautiful. Simply choose a character, cast aside your inhibitions, and begin a fantastic journey that will last as long as your make-up.

Using water-based paints, which wash out of clothes, hair, and face with just soap and water, you can build up layers of color to give a light, smooth "mask" that represents the character of your choice. A professional make-up artist takes you through the basic techniques, such as sponging and stippling, and then presents a stunning range of original designs, each clearly illustrated step–by–step.

If you do not want to paint your entire face, you could have just a small motif painted on your cheek; you can copy one of the cheek designs illustrated or think up one of your own. If you want to try something different again, this book also reveals the secrets of the gory world of special effects–shock your family and friends with a scab or open cut.

Whether you want to imitate, entertain, frighten, or celebrate, you can achieve it all with face painting. This book contains more than a dozen amazingly original designs for parties, special occasions, and Halloween - from cowboys to clowns, pirates to pumpkins, black cats to black eyes.

Happy painting!

ABOVE: Nadia Strahan making up as Bombalurina in Andrew Lloyd Webber's musical Cats.

ABOVE: Red is a significant colour for many tribes. It is mostly connected with blood, life, energy, success and well being. Upon marriage, women of many Asian and Middle Eastern countries, for example Bahrein, tint their hands and feet with red henna to invite success and good health to the home.

Equipment

For the designs in this book you will need the following:

EQUIPMENT

Aqua-Colours (water-based
  paints in a range of colours)
Black eye pencil
Bran flakes or cornflakes
Brushes
Cotton swabs
Derma Wax (or "nose putty")
Fake blood
Glitter gel for skin
Grey eye pencil
Hair brush & comb
Hair clips/hair band
Hair gel
Hairspray
Lead pencil
Mirror
Palette knife/spatula
Soap
Sponges
Tissues
Toothpick/orange stick
Towel
Tracing paper (or greaseproof
  paper)
Water
Water jar

Note: All the paints recommended
in this book are professional Aqua-
Colours. These are specially
formulated for use on skin, are non-
toxic and have been carefully tested.
However, if you suspect that your
model might have sensitive skin,
test the paint on the inside of the
model's wrist before you begin. If
there is no reaction after an hour or
two you should be safe to proceed.

Aqua-Colours

The main advantages of using
professional Aqua-Colours are that
they cover the skin well, yet only
need a thin layer of paint to do so.
They are available in a huge range of
colours that can be mixed easily and
dry very quickly on the skin,
enabling other colours to be added
almost immediately.

Because Aqua-Colours are water
based they are easily removed by
washing with ordinary soap and
water, and can also be used on the
hair for the same reason.

Aqua-Colours are inexpensive and
can be bought individually or in
palettes of 6 or 12 colours.
Fluorescent colours are also
available.

Brushes and Sponges

Special make-up sponges can be
bought from most drug stores,
but an ordinary bath sponge will do
the job just as well, if not better
sometimes.

A professional "stipple" sponge is
good for applying beard stubble, but
a plastic pan scourer will produce the
same effect.

A selection of quality brushes are
essential for a good make-up. The
most useful are: No. 2 for eye-lining
and fine detail; No. 6 for lips and
eyes; 6mm (¼in) domed for
highlights and blending; 12mm
(½in) domed for painting large areas
and for blending.

The best type of brushes are
sable, although other, cheaper types
can be used instead. Sable brushes

ABOVE: Equipment for achieving special effects.

are worth the extra initial expense because they are versatile and long lasting. Look after them carefully by washing them gently with soap and water after each session, then lubricating the hairs with a touch of cold cream. Your local art shop will be a good source of brushes.

Preparation Tips

☞ Set out all your materials and equipment in front of you so that you can see at a glance what you need.

☞ Lay out a towel or cloth to protect the table or work surface.

☞ Keep a waste bin or carrier bag handy to hold dirty tissues etc. and keep the work area clear.

☞ Try to ensure that your model sits on a seat that is high enough for you to work comfortably without straining your back.

☞ Have a mirror close at hand, preferably standing in front of you, so that you can check that your make-up design is balanced and the colours are evenly applied.

☞ Before you start, wrap a towel round your model's shoulders to protect the clothes.

☞ Keep the model's hair off the face with hair clips or a hair band.

☞ Have a good supply of cotton swabs handy for blending colours and erasing any smudges.

☞ Most important of all, work out your designs beforehand using a copy of the make-up chart on page 9. It is much better to make your mistakes on paper rather than a model's face! The chart will also be a useful record for future use.

Application Tips

☞ Always begin with a clean, dry face.

☞ For some designs you might find it helpful to sketch the outline onto the face first using grey eye pencil.

☞ When a full white base is required, try to apply it as thinly as possible while still achieving good coverage – this will avoid muddiness when other colours are added.

☞ Do not apply glitter too close to the eyes.

☞ When using Derma Wax (or nose putty) don't handle it for too long or it will become too sticky to use.

☞ Fake blood can be darkened by adding a little instant coffee, and can be made less orange or pink by adding a touch of green.

☞ Fake blood can stain clothing – take great care with it.

☞ When painting animal faces, it often helps to keep a photograph of the animal nearby. This will inspire you to imitate the real thing as accurately as possible.

☞ Keep each sponge for one colour only – washing sponges between colours takes up too much time.

☞ Change the water often.

☞ Always apply the lightest colours first, then progress to the darker ones.

☞ Wait until the previous colour is dry before applying the next one.

☞ Blend colours with a clean, damp brush or by stippling with a barely damp sponge.

☞ Take extra care when working near the eyes. If possible, ask the model to keep their eyes closed until you have finished.

☞ Always apply make-up with as much care as possible. Do not rush – the features will become ill-defined and uneven. Symmetrical shapes and neat lines are the essence of a good make-up. Practice makes perfect!

Basic Techniques

Applying a Base

TIP: Use a damp sponge to apply a full-face base. It is much quicker and gives a smoother finish than a brush. To avoid streaks or patchiness, make sure the sponge is not too wet.

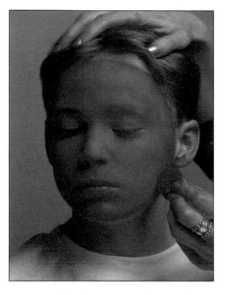

3 Blend an orange border into the yellow by lightly dabbing ("stippling") along the adjoining edge with a barely damp sponge.

TIP: Dark skins can sometimes be difficult to cover. Stipple the base colour over the entire face with a barely damp sponge. Metallic colours can be substituted, and look terrific. They also act as a primer onto which you can apply your base colour.

4 The finished duotone base.

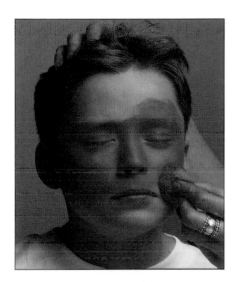

1 If you want a duotone base, always apply the lightest colour first – yellow in this case.

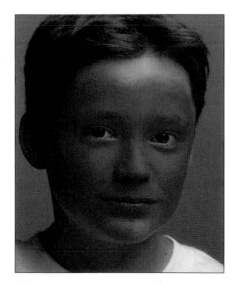

2 The yellow base reaches almost to the hairline.

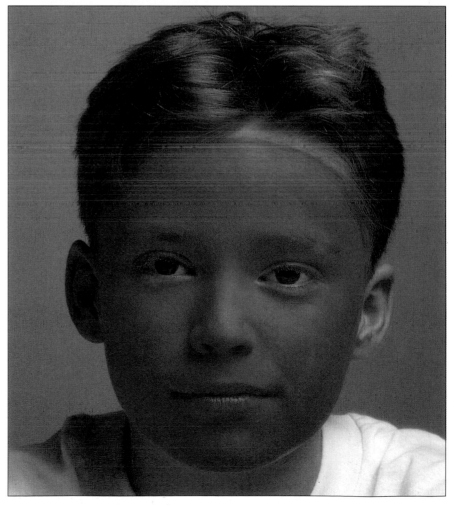

Painting the Eyes

T I P : Always take great care when painting anywhere near the eye. Most of the faces in this book have been designed so that the models can keep their eyes closed throughout the whole procedure. If you need to get closer to the bottom eye-line, ask the model to look up and away from the brush as you do so.

Method 1

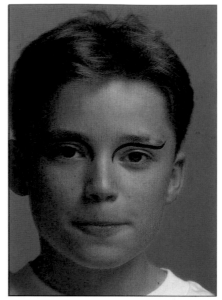

1 This method is ideal for very young children because it starts beside the nose and sweeps across the brow without actually touching the eye.

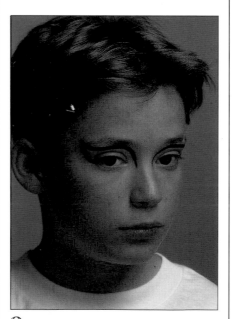

2 You can enhance the effect by simply bringing the end of the line down to meet the outer corner of the eye.

Method 2

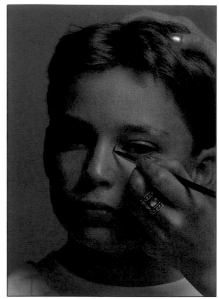

1 For a more elaborate image, use a thin brush and start the top line just below the inner corner of the eye.

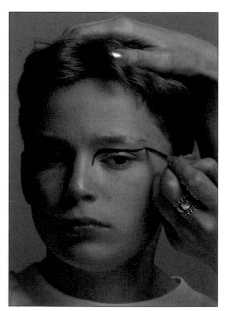

2 Take the line across the eyelid, winging it up slightly at the end.

Method 3

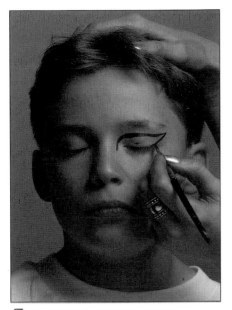

3 Bring the end of the top line down to the outer corner of the eye.

5 Start the bottom line at the inner corner and sweep it beneath the lower lashes to join the outer corner of the top lid.

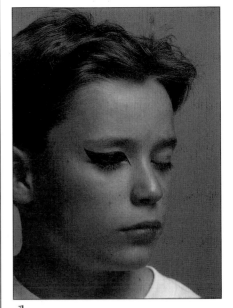

1 Shape the top lid using the method described previously.

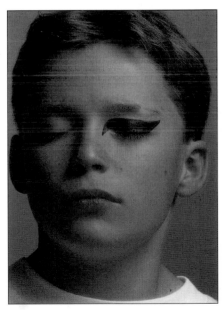

4 Fill in the outlined area in black.

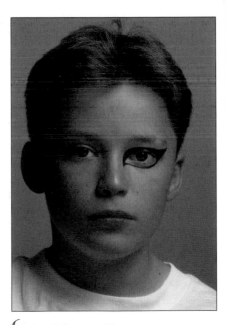

6 The finished effect.

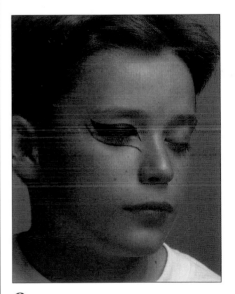

2 Start the lower line below the inner corner and sweep it up, following the direction of the top lid, to finish parallel to but not touching the top line. The space between the two lines can be emphasised with a slick of white paint.

☞ This "open-ended" technique is often used in the theatre because it makes the eyes appear larger.

Five O'Clock Shadow

1 To create an unshaven look, use a small coarse sponge to stipple black/brown paint gently over the beard and moustache area of the face.

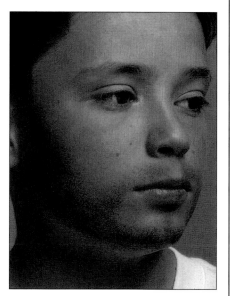

2 The finished effect.

TIP: Build up the depth of colour very gradually. Tap the sponge on the back of your hand before each application of colour to remove any excess paint. If any areas start to look too dark, stipple them lightly with a paler colour.

Eyebrows

A change of eyebrow shape can transform a face into a multitude of different characters. Think about the type of personality you are trying to convey. Make faces in the mirror – of laughter, anger, sadness – and see what happens to your features. Build up a repertoire of shapes based on what you observe.

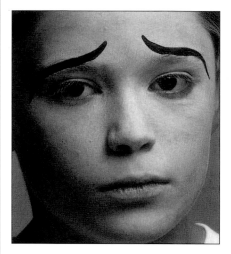

1. Sad.

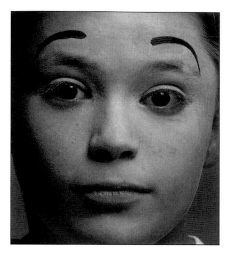

2. Surprised.

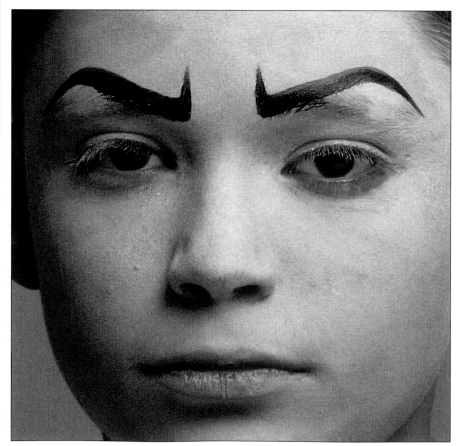

3. Cruel.

Using a Make-up Chart – A Finished Example

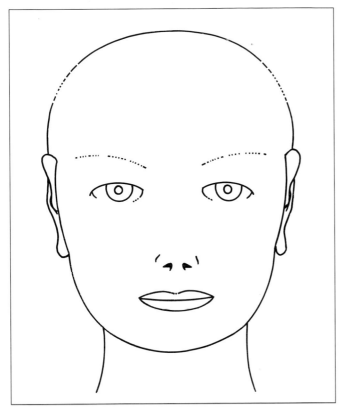

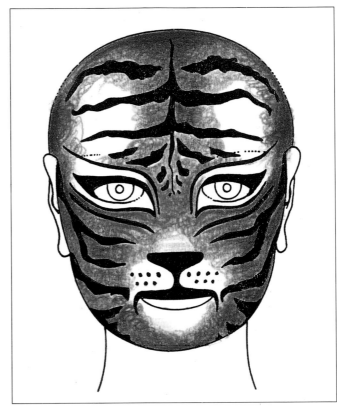

1 You can photocopy this blank chart to help you plan your own creations.

2 Fill in the design with paints, felt tips or coloured pencils.

3 Keep referring to your chart as you apply the make-up.

Tiger

1 Apply a base of yellow with orange on the outer edges. Stipple the colours together with a sponge.

2 Stipple on white patches around the mouth and above the eyebrows. Paint the eyes in black, starting just below the inner corner; take the colour across the lid and wing the line up slightly just past the outer corner of the eye. Paint the lower eyeline below the lashes, following the curve of the top line but leaving the outer end open.

The tiger's nose should be extended a little way onto the cheek.

3 For the tiger's stripes, use a narrow brush to paint black lines across the forehead. Finish one side of the face first, then copy the design onto the other side to keep the pattern symmetrical.

4 The finished tiger. Because the markings are so strong, there is no need to add whiskers — these would only clutter the face and spoil the effect.

Dog

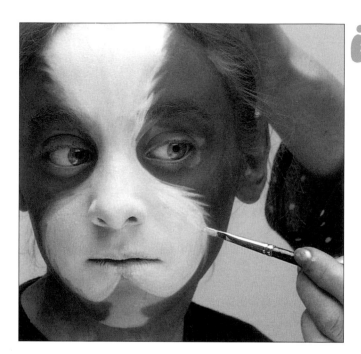

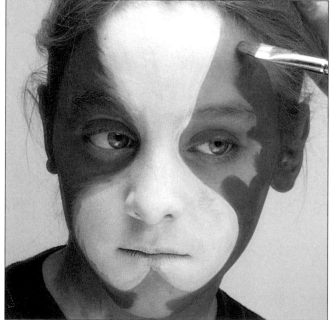

1 Using a flat, wide brush, paint this white shape down the centre of the face.

2 Fill in around the white with a mid-brown.

3 Soften the line where the two colours meet by feathering the white onto the brown with a very fine brush.

4 Paint the eyes in dark brown, using jagged, uneven brush strokes.

5 Use black for the mouth, extending the line beyond the corners of the mouth before dropping it down sharply to the chin. Paint the tip of the nose black and add some black whisker spots.

6 The drooping tongue is dark red. Fleck the eye areas with red and yellow to highlight them.

Black Cat

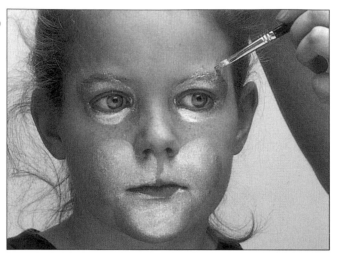

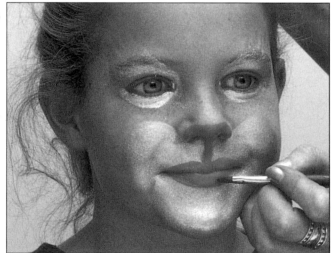
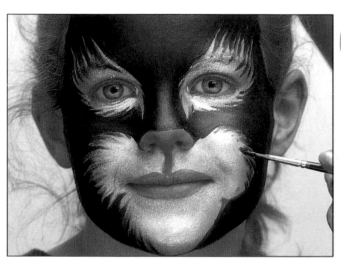

1 Paint silver around the mouth, chin and eyes, making these areas slightly larger than they will eventually be.

2 Square off the end of the nose in pink, and apply the same colour to the lips.

3 Carefully paint round the silver features in black, then fill in the rest of the face.

4 Using a fine brush and sharp, delicate strokes, feather the black paint onto the silver to give a softer, more textured effect.

5 Add black whisker spots, followed by white whiskers and white eyebrow details. Because the paint is easily removed by washing, the colours can be extended into the hair to complete the make-up.

6 The finished black cat.

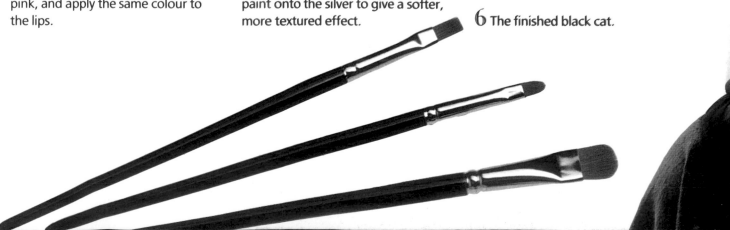

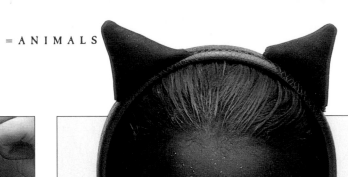

Eyes on Eyelids

Ask the model to close her eyes, then paint the upper eyelids yellow, outline the eye socket with a thin line of black and paint a black iris in the centre.

Funny Clown

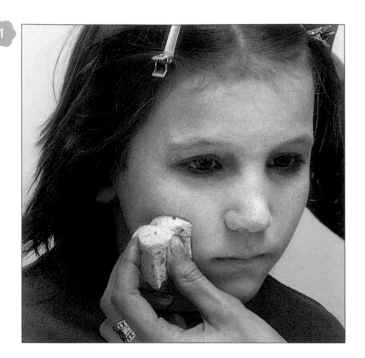

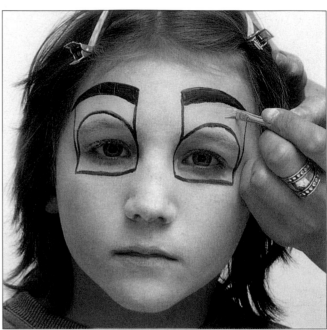

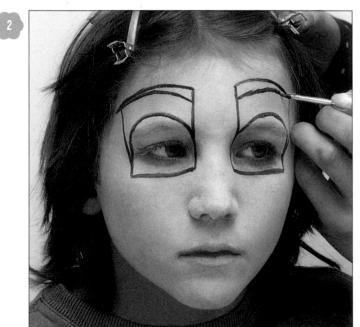

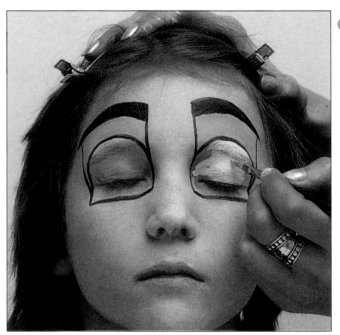

1 Cover the whole face in white paint using a sponge. Stipple lightly over any patches that seem streaky to make a really smooth finish.

2 Draw in the main eye shapes with a very fine brush, and add the eyebrows.

3 Fill in the eyebrows in black. The space underneath each one is filled in with blue.

4 Cover the main eye area carefully in white.

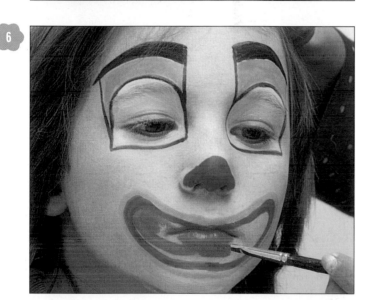

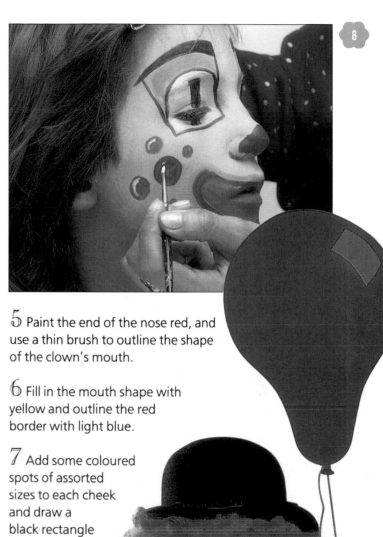

5 Paint the end of the nose red, and use a thin brush to outline the shape of the clown's mouth.

6 Fill in the mouth shape with yellow and outline the red border with light blue.

7 Add some coloured spots of assorted sizes to each cheek and draw a black rectangle in the centre of each eyelid.

8 The nose and cheek spots will benefit from some white highlights.

Pumpkin

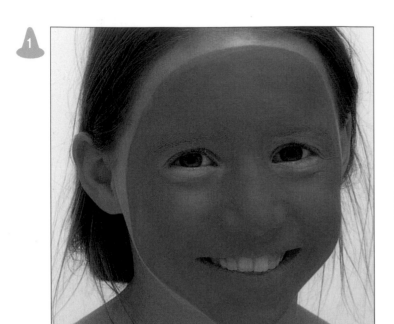

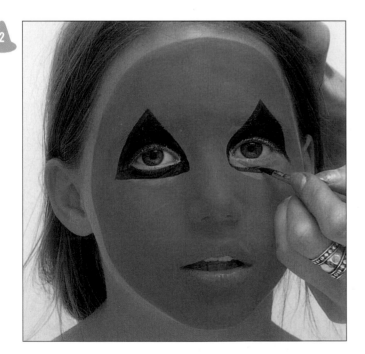

1 Paint a large orange circle over the whole face, filling in the colour with a sponge.

2 Add a black triangle over each eye, using a fine brush. Extend the points of the triangle below the line of the lower lid and carefully fill in the centre leaving a margin around the eye.

3 Paint another triangle on the tip of the nose and extend the sides out onto the cheeks.

4 Outline a huge smile in black and make the top edge a zig-zag line.

5 Fill in the whole mouth shape with black.

6 Design a small green stalk in the middle of the forehead and run some segment lines down from it, following the curve of the orange outline.

Skull

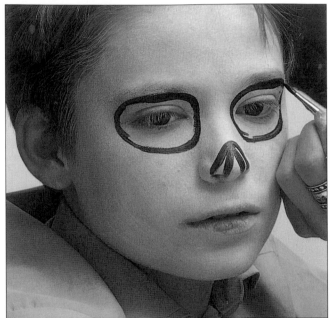

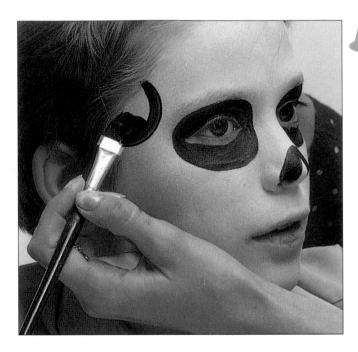

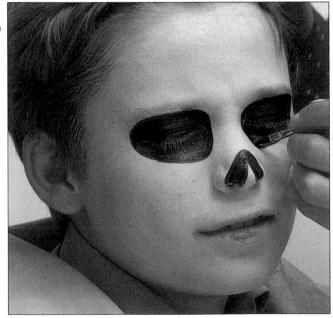

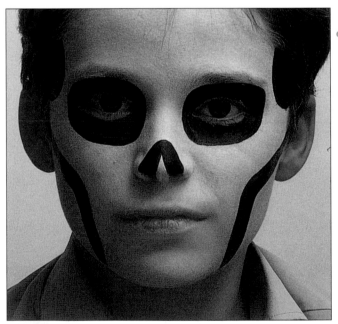

1 Cover the whole face in white using a sponge. Draw in the outlines for the nose and eye sockets in black.

2 Fill in these areas in black, leaving a small segment of white showing at the centre of the nose.

3 Feel for the model's temple hollows and emphasise them by painting a black semicircle over each one.

4 Feel for the cheekbones and paint along the underside, stopping approximately level with the centre of the eye. Then drop the line downwards to the jawline. Fill in the area behind this line with black.

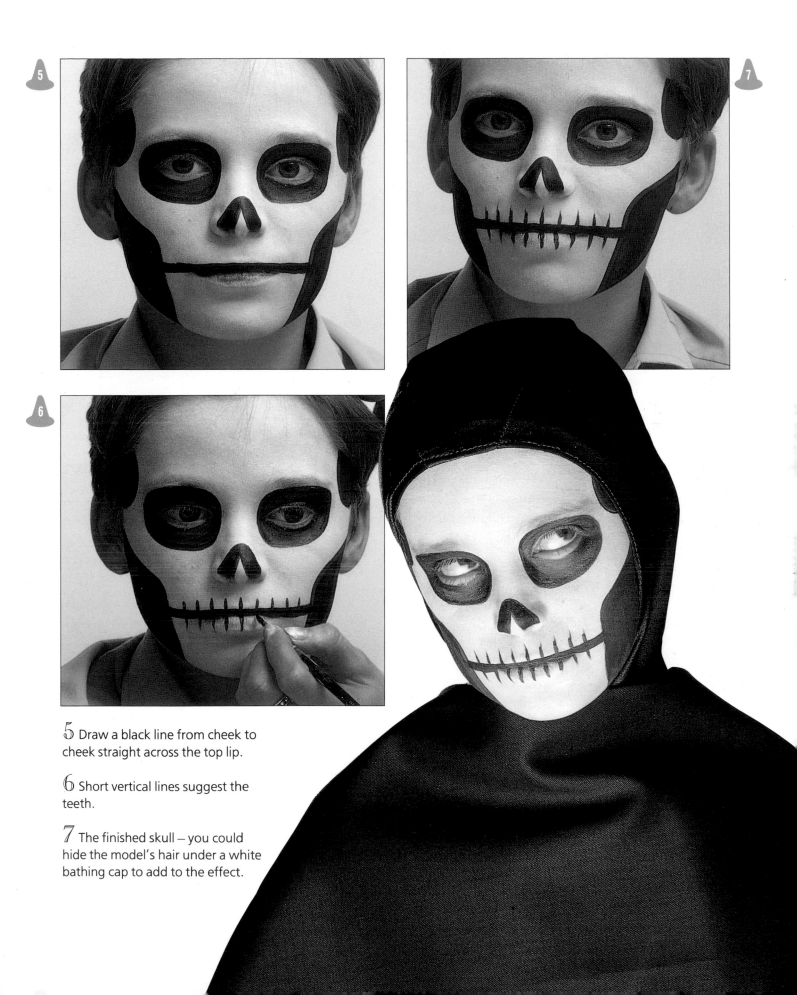

5 Draw a black line from cheek to cheek straight across the top lip.

6 Short vertical lines suggest the teeth.

7 The finished skull – you could hide the model's hair under a white bathing cap to add to the effect.

Dracula

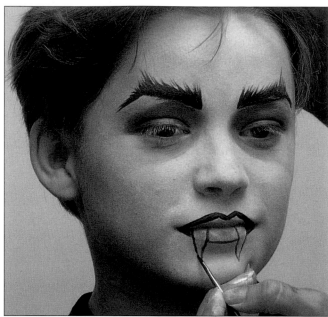

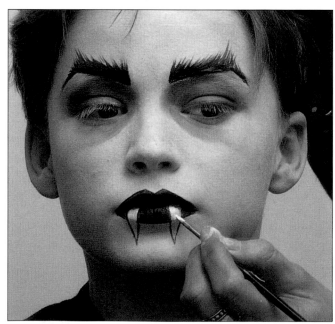

1 Cover the face with white, gently stippling over any patchy areas with a sponge. Add some angular black eyebrows, brushing upwards with light feathery brushstrokes.

2 Paint some grey over the top eyelid, round the inner corner of the eye and along the lower socket line. Blend the edges with a clean damp brush.

3 Draw the outline of long pointed fangs over the bottom lip, using a fine brush or a sharp black eye pencil.

4 Fill in the fangs in white and the surrounding lips in black.

5 Use a brush or cotton swab to smudge some red paint along the lower eyelash line. The model should look up and away from you while you do this. Shade the cheek hollows with light grey using a sponge or a brush. Powder eye shadow could be used instead of paint, but powder colours are usually less dense than paint and do not last so long.

6 Add trickles of blood from the fangs and corners of the mouth.

Cowboy

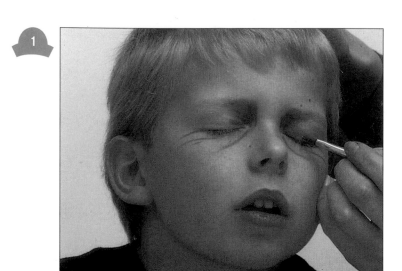

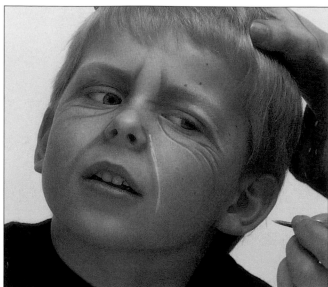

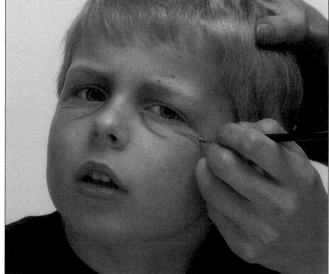

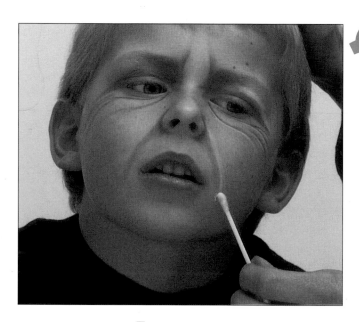

1 Using a thin brush and mid-brown paint, shade the eyelid and the inner corner of the eye, blending the colour down the sides of the nose slightly. Add a subtle line of colour to the lower part of the eye socket.

2 Add some wrinkle lines in their natural positions: downwards from the outer corner of the eye, from the nose down to the corners of the mouth, in the crease of the chin and across the forehead, as well as two vertical frown lines above the eyebrows.

3 Highlight the lines and wrinkles by painting a little white alongside them. To make the eyelids look droopy, paint a white diagonal line along the fold of the upper lid, starting at the eyebrow and ending below the outer corner of the eye.

4 Blend any hard edges using a slightly dampened cotton swab.

5 Create an unshaven look by stippling the beard and moustache area with a coarse sponge and some brown paint. Build up the effect gradually, using only a small amount of color. Dab the sponge on the back of your hand to remove any excess paint. Darken the eyebrows if necessary. This subtle make-up will enhance any cowboy fancy dress costume.

Pirate

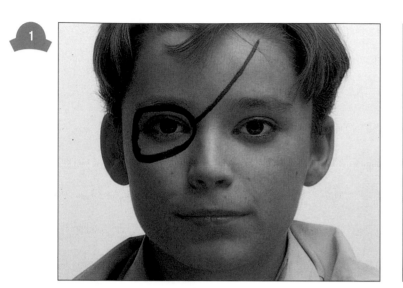

1 Draw the outline of the eye patch with a fine brush.

2 Fill in the outline with black and draw in the ties.

3 Create an unshaven look by stippling black paint gently onto the lower face with a sponge (see page 25 for full intructions).

TIP: Build up the colour gradually and don't overdo it.

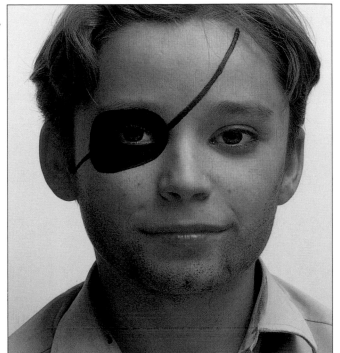

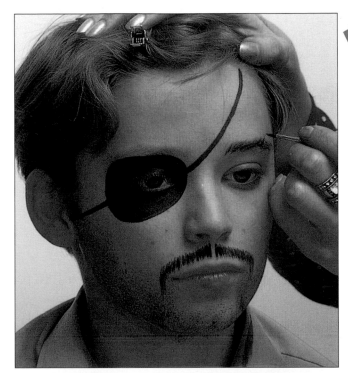

4 A realistic five o'clock shadow is beginning to emerge.

5 Paint on the moustache with a very fine brush using small sharp strokes.

6 Emphasise the model's eyebrows using the same sharp brush technique.

7 Create a scar by painting a thin dark red line and outlining it in white to achieve a 3-D effect. Paint on a few drops of fake blood.

Cheek Designs

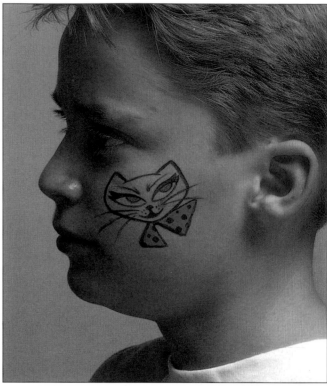

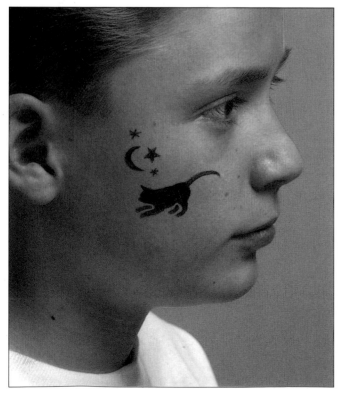

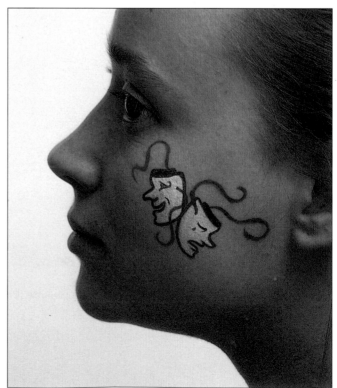

These little designs are quick and fun to do. Of course they don't have to go on your cheek – you could decorate your arms, legs, even your feet. Anything goes! The only basic rule to remember is that once you have drawn out the main outline, always apply the lightest colours first.

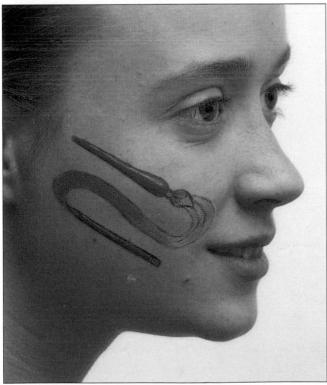

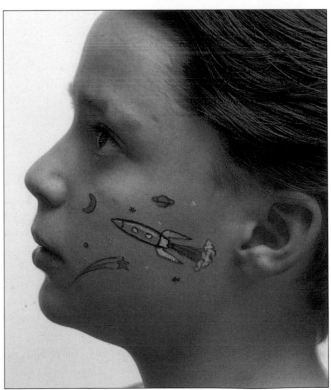

Open Cut

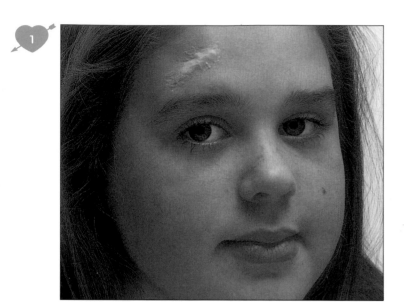

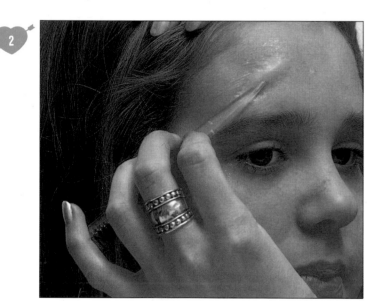

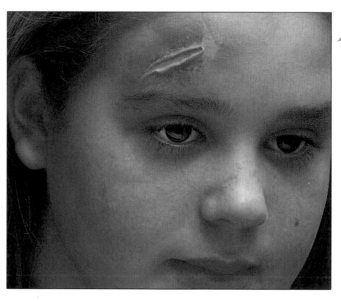

TIP: Avoid handling the wax too much, as it will become too soft and sticky to work with.

1 Mould a small amount of wax into the basic shape of the cut you are going to create. Press it gently onto the skin.

2 With a spatula or the back of your fingernail, shape and thin out the edges of the wax so that they blend onto the skin.

TIP: A tiny touch of cold cream will help to smooth out the edges.

3 With your finger or a small brush, lightly colour the wax and the surrounding area in dark red. A hint

of dark blue can be added to suggest bruising. The colours will look more effective if they are left mottled rather than blended together too much.

4 Pick away the wax to form the cut, using either the end of a spatula or brush, or a toothpick or orange stick.

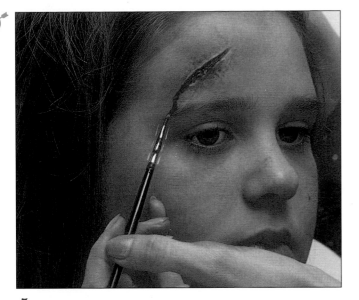

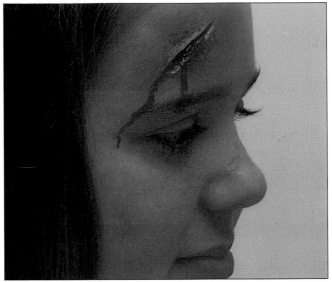

5 Line the centre of the cut with dark red using a fine brush. A few drops of fake blood help to make the cut look real.

TIP: If the fake blood appears too pink or orange mix in a little grey paint.

6 The finished wound.

Scab

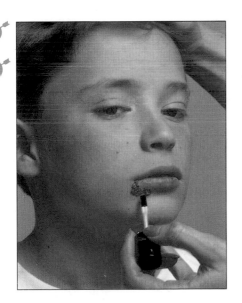

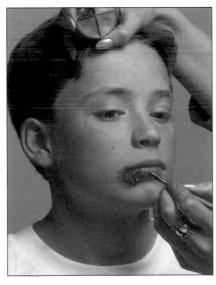

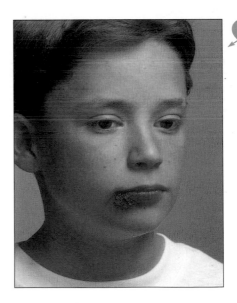

1 Crush a bran flake or cornflake into small pieces and stick them onto the skin using a tiny dab of surgical or water-soluble adhesive.

2 Discolour the area around the flakes by applying dark red with a brush, adding a few spots of grey/ green here and there. Blend the edges of the colours into the skin with a cotton swab.

3 The finished scab.

TIP: The same method can be used with puffed rice to make very realistic warts and blisters.

Black Eye

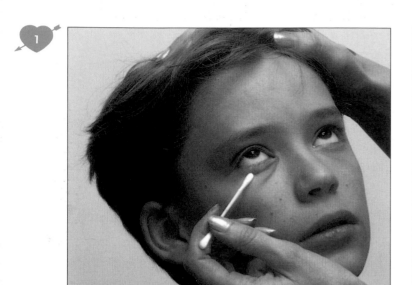

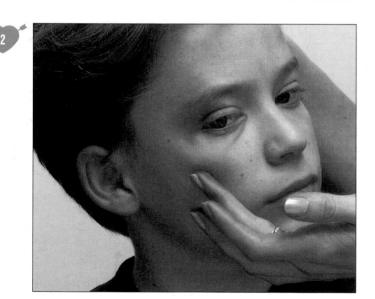

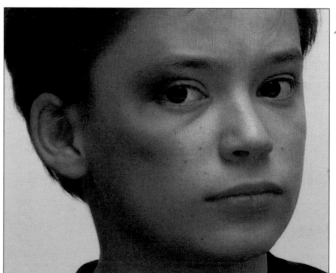

1 Mix dark red paint with a dash of grey and dab the colour over the outer eyelid and brow bone with your finger or a sponge. Using a brush, paint into the lower eye socket line at both the inner and outer corners of the eye. Blend the edges carefully with a cotton swab.

2 Feel for the cheekbone and dab some colour along the underside, fading out towards the temple.

3 Go back over the same areas with a touch of dark blue, allowing the colour to be a little heavier around the outer corner of the eye.

4 The finished black eye looks painfully realistic.

TIP: To make an eye look bloodshot, paint red along the inner rim.

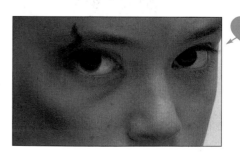

5 For even more realism, add a small jagged red scar painted just above the eyebrow.